ROMANUS CESSARIO, O.P.

COMPASSIONATE
BLOOD

Publisher: Pierre-Marie Dumont
Editor: Romain Lizé
Copyediting: Susan Needham
Iconography: Isabelle Mascaras
Layout and cover: Gauthier Delauné
Production: Thierry Dubus, Florence Bellot
Proofreading: Claire Gilligan

Front cover: *Saint Catherine of Siena* (1746), Giambattista Tiepolo (1696-1770),
Kunsthistorisches Museum, Vienna, Austria. © FineArtImages / Leemage.
Back cover: *Saint Catherine of Siena Meditating* (c. 1593), Francesco Eugenio Vanni
(c. 1563-1610), Louvre Museum, Paris, France. © RMN-GP / Michel Urtado.

Printed by Imprimerie Marquis, Canada
Edition number: MGN 17007
ISBN: 978-1-941709-38-2

ROMANUS CESSARIO, O.P.

COMPASSIONATE BLOOD

Catherine of Siena on the Passion

MAGNIFICAT

Paris • New York • Oxford • Madrid

CONTENTS

PREFACE

Good Friday fell on April 22 in 2011. At noon on New York's Upper East Side, I began to preach a series of conferences according to the customary style of the three hours' reflection on the Passion and Death of our Lord Jesus Christ. The Catholic Church makes use of this devotion in order to focus the attention of people everywhere on a moment of unsurpassable importance. It is the moment when Christ's Death on the cross brings salvation to the whole world.

The church where these conferences were preached bears the name of Saint Catherine of Siena, a 14th-century mystic and advisor to popes. This patronage explains the book's sources, whereas the occasion explains its focus on Christ's last words from the cross. I am grateful to Reverend Jordan Kelly, o.p., who held the post of pastor, for his kind invitation to preach these conferences.

Since its arrival in the United States twenty years ago, MAGNIFICAT has become for more than a quarter of a million people a standard feature of Catholic daily life and worship. This small book, which may serve as a companion to the monthly journal, commemorates the score of years that MAGNIFICAT has provided spiritual enrichment to American Catholics. Gratitude is also due Messrs. Romain Lizé and Axel d'Epinay for their roles in making the miracle of MAGNIFICAT happen. I dedicate the book to Ambassador Mary Ann Glendon, a valiant and gracious woman who, like Catherine of Siena, has both advised popes and served the Holy See with passionate zeal.

INTRODUCTION

During the Lent of 1380, the year in which Saint Catherine of Siena died in Rome, she walked daily to Saint Peter's Basilica.[1] This Lenten practice appears all the more remarkable when we consider that toward the end of February of that year, Catherine Benincasa had lost the normal use of her legs. What, we might ask, would have prompted Catherine to make this sacrifice? She supplies the answer in a letter from the same period: "Then God imposed this obedience on me, that during this entire time of Lent I should have the whole family sacrifice their desires and celebrate before him alone in this way for the holy Church. And I should attend Mass every morning at dawn—which, as you know, is impossible for me, but in obedience to God everything has been possible.[2]" As Raymond of Capua explains in his *Life* of the saint, Catherine's "family" comprises "her children in Christ, those spiritual sons and daughters of hers whom she had with her" in Rome.[3] Those blessed souls who take up the present volume should consider themselves among those whom Catherine of Siena welcomes into her "family," that is, they should think of themselves as numbered among her spiritual sons and daughters. As Catherine's spiritual children, we petition the saint to guide our reflections on those mysteries that she herself most loved and that, we are told, she bore in her own flesh: the mysteries of the Passion and the Death of our Lord Jesus Christ.[4]

In the *Letters* and in the *Dialogue*, her principal writings, Catherine of Siena describes the transformation that Christian faith and Baptism accomplish in the Catholic believer.[5] In one especially poetic passage, she writes to a knight-monk. His name was Nicholas di Strozzi, and he was a prior in one of the military orders that flourished during the Middle Ages. These knight-monks aimed to combine the virtues of chivalry with the ideals of asceticism. To Prior Nicholas, then, Catherine writes:

> Our King [she refers to Christ] behaves like a true knight who perseveres in battle until the enemies are defeated.... [W]ith unarmed

hand, nailed fast to the cross, he defeated the prince of the world, with the wood of the holy cross as his mount. This knight of ours came armed with the breastplate of Mary's flesh, flesh that bore the blows to make up for our wickedness. The helmet on his head is the painful crown of thorns, driven right into his brain. The sword at his side is the wound of his side, revealing to us the secret of his heart; it is a sword with a point of light that ought to pierce our inmost heart with the force of love. The staff in his hand is there in mockery. And the gloves on his hands and spurs on his feet are the scarlet wounds in the hands and feet of this gentle loving Word. [6]

What do we learn from this description of the suffering Christ? What does Catherine teach us about the transformation that brings the world stillness on Good Friday from noon until three o'clock? The answer is simple: We discover that because of his enormous love, Christ's sufferings and Death cause the transformation of all that exists, the transformation we call Christian salvation. "What held him nailed firm and fast to the cross?" Catherine inquires. "Neither the nails nor the cross, which were not capable of holding the God-Man, but the bond of love for the Father's honor and our salvation."[7] "What armed him?" Catherine further asks. Her answer: "Love." The transformation that Catherine announces is one that creates in those persons who remain united with Christ a new ground for love, a new sort of loving. We call this freely bestowed transformation the gift of divine grace, both habitual and actual. The transformation affects both our persons and our actions.

In order to benefit from this meditation on Christ's Passion, the benevolent reader is invited graciously to take Catherine of Siena as guide and companion. During those precious moments of retreat from the world's busyness and distractions, moments that each Christian must daily find time to allow, the reader should become a member of Catherine's "family," her *bella brigata*, her beautiful bunch. Those who make this choice place themselves under the sign of Catherine's motherhood, her spiritual maternity, her sisterly instrumentality. Saint Catherine of Siena surely will receive each Christian and will make each one her own.

"In my beginning is my end," as T. S. Eliot remarks in the second of his *Four Quartets*, "East Coker."[8] We begin our meditation on Christ's compassionate blood, shed at the end of his earthly life, but which serves as the beginning for every Christian's autobiography. In a sense, every Christian is born anew on the day Christ died. The shedding of his compassionate blood causes the transformation that once and for all enters our world on that blessed day that the Church everywhere reveres as "Good." Good Friday. What matters most? That this grace-fueled transformation envelop us. The assurance of a good outcome, however, is best founded upon the aid of an experienced spiritual guide. Catherine, a Dominican, a Doctor of the Church, is such a guide. Catherine, our sister; Catherine, our mother.

To help focus these meditations, I have chosen seven mysteries of Catholic life upon which Catherine of Siena loved to meditate, mysteries that she still loves in heaven. First, Catherine loves the Savior; second, she loves his cross; third, she loves his Mother, Mary. Fourth, Catherine loves the consolation that God bestows in Jesus and Mary; fifth, she loves Christ's thirst for souls, his zeal for our salvation; sixth, she loves the pope, the vicar of Christ; and finally, seventh, Catherine, our sister, loves the priests of Christ's Church. Why these seven loves, these seven mystical loves? The answer comes easily. Catherine loves all those whom these mysteries in one way or another redeem. Each of these mysteries represents the great event of what Catherine calls Christ's "compassionate blood." How are we to understand this event? Catherine answers this question when she addresses Christ with these words: "Oh compassionate blood, through you was distilled compassionate mercy!"[9] So, come now! Let Catherine's loves inflame each reader's heart. Think of her as "Catherine, My Mother," to borrow the title of the television play by Dominican Father Dominic Rover.[10] Let her mediate Christ's own compassion for us sinners.

THE SAVIOR

"Ah, dearest father, this is what gentle First Truth is teaching you and leaving you as a commandment: to love God above all things and your neighbor as yourself. He gave you the example, hanging on the wood of the most holy cross. While the Jews cried, 'Crucify him!' he cried out humbly, meekly: 'Father, forgive those who are crucifying me, because they don't know what they are doing!' Look at his boundless charity!"[11] For Catherine, Christ's words from the cross startlingly express sentiments of forgiveness, even as they signal the universal reconciliation that his Death accomplishes. She plumbs the depth of this mystery: "Then Jesus said, 'Father, forgive them, they know not what they do'" (Lk 23:34).

These words from the lips of Christ express the reason for the very existence of his cross. They confirm the reason or motive for the Incarnation of the Son of God, an Incarnation that finds its most cogent and scripturally warranted explanation in the universal need for forgiveness that the human race inherits from Adam, and that the members of the race have ratified by their sins. From the cross, "gentle First Truth," as Catherine addresses Christ, announces the divine mission that on Calvary he completes.

Should we be surprised that Christ's words from the cross instruct us? Of course not. He speaks words from the cross to teach the world about the mystery that unfolds before the eyes of those whom God calls to belief. Christ preaches to us from the cross. Those who hear his "homilies" and believe them find life. So Catherine frequently compares the cross of Christ to a preacher's pulpit. The several words that Christ speaks from the cross fit together to produce a well-constructed sermon; they form a divine instruction that both provokes and moves us. Christ sets an example for all future preachers of divine Truth: the words that come from the Church's authentic preachers should first instruct people in the Truth and then excite them to embrace what they believe. This compassionate word from the cross announces the divine forgiveness that on Calvary spills out upon the world like a burst bag of gold coins. Christ's forgiveness embraces all time and space, and it makes Calvary the fulcrum of the universe that men and angels inhabit. So the Fathers of the Church placed a skull at the foot of Christ's cross, a skull that (they held) belonged to Adam, the first human being, in whom all the others have sinned.

The temporal consequences of Adam's original sin are passed on to his descendants, even those redeemed by Christ. No one escapes. Who are his descendants? The human race. Is God fair? Dare we ask the question? Though, if for apologetic reasons we must ask it, then the answer comes easily: Grace is a gift. Without the grace of original justice, the human person falls back on its own natural propensities, as does the human community. Man then finds himself "subject to ignorance, suffering, and the dominion of death; and inclined to sin—an inclination to evil called 'concupiscence.'"[12] Only the Blessed Virgin Mary, by the special privilege of her Immaculate Conception, escapes this original sin and the moral weaknesses that it leaves in us. For the rest of us, there remains spiritual engagement, a spiritual combat that the sacraments of new life equip us to undertake. Baptism, Confirmation, and Marriage for most; Baptism, Confirmation, and Holy Orders for the priest, whose special vocation in the Church calls him to a specific holiness. Catherine of Siena never tires of reminding her correspondents about the several recognized vocations in the Church and the distinctive energies they require. In short, Catherine calls the members of the Church away from a sinful lethargy, thereby encouraging renewed spiritual energy to spring up in every person.

We should not take Catherine's gentle urging as being offered *pro forma*. It remains as opportune today as it was in the second half of the 14th century, a time when the Church underwent severe trials. The 20th-century Catholic writer Flannery O'Connor puts it best: "Redemption is meaningless unless there is cause for it in the actual life we live, and for the last few centuries there has been operating in our culture the secular belief that there is no such cause."[13] The cause to which Miss O'Connor refers occupies its own place in the spiritual doctrine of Catherine of Siena. In a letter to an Augustinian priest, Giovanni Tantucci, who would deliver the eulogy at Catherine's funeral in 1380, our saint explains: "[S]in alone is evil…. It was the cause of Christ's Death…. Only sin is evil, not other things."[14] As we reflect upon the Passion of Christ and his compassionate blood, bear in mind that no entrance into the mystery of salvation exists that does not include a frank recognition of the evil of sin. Even the poet and deathbed Catholic Oscar Wilde, while serving a jail sentence for his sinful crimes, wrote: "Ah! happy they whose hearts can break / And peace of pardon win! / How else may man make straight his plan / And cleanse his soul from Sin? / How else but through a broken heart / May Lord Christ enter in?"[15]

Not every citizen of the world sees things as clearly as does the author of *The Ballad of Reading Gaol*. It remains a general rule of thumb that people prefer to forget sin rather than to seek forgiveness for it. We can recognize this tendency in ourselves each time that we are tempted to make excuses for our sins, whether they rank as big or small. We also encounter other strategies that people adopt in order to absolve themselves from the sin that Adam's original sin introduced into the world. Even when people begin to suffer under the weight of their sins, they often turn to excuse-making and rationalization. "If only my husband were a better man...." "If only," says a priest, "I were not so busy, or bored, or bothered, then I could pray, or work, or find recollection." "If only the world were a fairer place to work in...." "If only other people would set better examples, but everybody does this or that." The list of excuses goes on and on. What makes these various strategies of self-deception so distressing is not the inescapable fact that the people who fabricate them remain set in their disorders. Rather, what makes the forgetfulness of sin so distressful is that it brings with it a forgetfulness of the gift of salvation, of the transformation that Christ's love brings about on the cross.

No need for discouragement! Catherine, when writing to the pope himself, found herself obliged to address this primordial temptation that afflicts every member of the Church. As her letters indicate, Catherine was given to provide spiritual consolation for every class of people. So to Pope Gregory XI, she wrote around Christmastime of 1376: "You will find peace and quiet and consolation in suffering when you see yourself conformed in that suffering with Christ crucified. And so, by enduring with Christ crucified, you will come with joy from much war into much peace."[16] Catherine's reference to "war" describes the political circumstances that Pope Gregory XI faced when he planned his return from France to Rome. She also had in mind what Saint Paul teaches in the Letter to the Romans: "For I know that good does not dwell in me, that is, in my flesh.... For I do not do the good I want, but I do the evil I do not want.... So, then, I discover the principle that when I want to do right, evil is at hand. For I take delight in the law of God, in my inner self, but I see in my members another principle at war with the law of my mind, taking me captive to the law of sin that dwells in my members" (Rom 7:18a, 19, 21-23). Only the God-Man can provide a universal remedy for this universal predicament. The Lord Jesus Christ alone can help us escape the internal conflict with which original sin burdens us. Catherine loves the Savior of the world. She loves Jesus Christ.

Christ's first word from the cross urges us to cultivate confidence in the divine mercy. When Christ forgives his executioners, he also addresses his words to the whole human race. No person on the planet can escape responsibility for Christ's Death. For in Adam, "all sinned" (Rom 5:12). Our guide, Catherine of Siena, strongly encourages us, just as a mother would urge her children to do the right thing, to hear Christ's word as an invitation. "Father, forgive them, they know not what they do" (Lk 23:34). Sweet Jesus invites us! Jesus Crucified invites us. Gentle First Truth invites us. Lord, have mercy on us!

SWEET
CROSS

Catherine once wrote to a certain woman, Nella Buonconti, a wife and mother who lived with her family in Pisa and whose son had extended hospitality to Catherine and her "family" during their stay in that northern Italian city. Here is what she said. "The sufferings of this life are not worth comparing with the future glory that God has prepared for those who reverence him and who with good patience endure the holy discipline imposed on them by divine Goodness. In their patience, these people are experiencing even in this life the earnest of eternal life."[17] Her words introduce an especially comforting word that Jesus spoke from the cross: "Then [the good thief] said, 'Jesus, remember me when you come into your kingdom.' He replied to him, 'Amen, I say to you, today you will be with me in Paradise'" (Lk 23:42-43). From what we can gather, the good thief, whom the tradition names Dismas, exhibited at the end of his life the workings of grace that Saint Paul would later describe in the eighth chapter of Romans: "I consider that the sufferings of this present time are as nothing compared with the glory to be revealed for us" (Rom 8:18). What, however, explains that only one of the two criminals who were crucified with Jesus received this remarkable grace to turn to him and to seek an "earnest of eternal life"?

The answer to this question is not found by examining the religious psychology of the good thief. We cannot discover the answer by looking at the sinner. As far as we know, both criminals had enthusiastically pursued their careers of thievery and, since being condemned, had been awaiting the day of their execution. One remained stoutly scornful; the other turned pleadingly to Jesus. What moved the good thief to make his plea? What explains his presumably sudden about-face? Why does Dismas utter the prayer that Christians repeat with earnestness even until the present day? "Jesus, remember me when you come into your kingdom" (Lk 23:42). To discover how it came to pass that an everyday thief became a good thief, we must consider two themes: first, the immensity of the divine goodness and, second, the efficacy of Christ's Death on a cross. These themes dominate the spiritual doctrine of Saint Catherine of Siena, as they do all spiritual instruction that depends on the thought of Saint Thomas Aquinas.

Look not at the good thief for an explanation of his conversion. Look rather at the source of all goodness and conversion and transformation in the world.[18] Look to the good God. At times of sin and other distresses, this invitation to embrace the divine goodness can challenge even the devout. Catherine, however, makes that embracing easy! Easy for the devout. Easy for the sinner. To another woman, one moreover who enjoyed a reputation for indulging worldly desires, Catherine felt compelled to explain the dynamics of the divine love. "But you will say to me," she wrote to Regina della Scala, "'Since I have no such love, and without it I am powerless, how can I get it?' I will tell you," Catherine continues. Her reply seems too simple for the theologically sophisticated to take it seriously, but Catherine's authority trumps such a phony demurral. "Love," explains Catherine, "is had only by loving. If you want love, you must begin by loving."[19] What a precious lesson to receive from our guide, our companion, our sister, our saint, Catherine of Siena: "Love is had only by loving." Is it not true? Do we not see this principle verified in the good thief's plea? Of course he had only a few minutes left for the miracle of love to work, but he took advantage of a privileged moment. We of course remain well advised not to wait as long as Dismas waited to live within the embrace of the divine goodness. But the mystery of the compassionate blood always works. It works whether one begins living the mystery at the start of life, in the middle of it, or even at the end. And thank God! Priests then are encouraged not to abandon the deathbeds of their parishioners. These Other Christs alone can authoritatively proclaim to the repentant sinner, "Today you will be with Christ in Paradise."

God never abandons us. The divine goodness remains present to us, always there to fill up what is empty and vacant in our lives. This assurance explains why Catherine instructs Regina della Scala that she should become accustomed to reflecting on her own nothingness.

"And once you see that of yourself you do not even exist," Catherine explains, "you will recognize and appreciate that God is the source of your existence and of every favor above and beyond that existence—God's graces and gifts both temporal and spiritual."[20] Instead of emphasizing the disjunctive conjunction either/or, Catherine prefers what Hans Urs von Balthasar later called "the catholic *and*."[21] Divine premotion *and* human freedom. Divine grace *and* human nature. God *and* the cross of God's only Son. "For without existence, we would not be able to receive any grace at all," Catherine writes to Regina. "So everything we have, everything we discover within ourselves, is indeed the gift of God's boundless goodness and charity."[22]

Catherine loves the cross of Christ. How many of her letters begin "In the name of Jesus Christ crucified"! Because she recognizes in Christ's Passion the expression of the divine love that sets in motion the new creation, Catherine reveres and cherishes Christ's cross. "When we see ourselves loved we love in return," she assures us.[23] On the cross, Christ exhibits the greatest possible love, so says Saint Thomas Aquinas.[24] Catherine calls the cross "love's fire"; fed in this fire, "we realize how loved we are when we see that we ourselves were the soil and the rock that held the standard of the most holy cross."[25] In other words, in order to appreciate the place that we poor sinners hold in the drama of Christ's Passion, we need first to find comfort from "love's fire," from the holy cross of sweet Jesus crucified. Like a little moth that can only find itself drawn to the fire that will consume it, the soul finds itself drawn to the cross. And what do we discover when we land close to "love's fire"? "That neither earth nor rock could have held the cross, nor could the cross or nails have held God's only-begotten Son, had not love held him fast."[26] Catherine's catechesis reaches its completion. What moved the good thief? Love. God's love. God's love shining through the human face of the Savior. Sweet Jesus. Jesus crucified.

The example of the good thief consoles the Christian people. We rejoice that God loves us because he is good, not because we are. We commit ourselves to a continuous enactment of the good thief's faith and hope and charity. "Remember me!" We recognize that the cross of Christ stands at the center of the universe: as the poet says, "At the still point of the turning world."[27] God never destroys the creatures that he has made, to whom he has given the borrowed existence of human life. At the same time, as the Church sings at the Easter Vigil, "Our birth would have been no gain, had we not been redeemed."[28] The good thief continues to assure us that our Redeemer still stands close by. Especially from his cross, Christ—with his divinely bestowed ability to behold the whole human race—loves us. And best of all, since in one unforgettable instance Christ himself answered the good thief's prayer, each one of us may, with believers of all dispositions, still find great comfort in repeating his petition, "Jesus, remember me when you come into your kingdom" (Lk 23:42).

MOTHER
MARY

"Ah, son given me by that sweet mother Mary! I don't want you to yield to weariness or confusion, no matter what may trouble your spirit."[29] Thus writes Catherine of Siena to her Dominican biographer and spiritual counselor, Raymond of Capua—an Italian city located in the Campania—while the brave priest was sojourning in Avignon.[30] Nothing happens by accident. The Blessed Virgin Mary herself earlier had revealed to Catherine that this Dominican priest, Raymond delle Vigne, would serve as her confessor and guide. So much did Catherine recognize in Raymond a spiritual companion confided to her by the Blessed Virgin Mary, that she developed the practice of addressing him not by his ordinary name, Raymond, but rather by the name of the Beloved Disciple, "John"— Saint John the Evangelist, the disciple to whom the dying Christ had confided his Mother.[31]

We read in the Evangelist's account of Christ's Passion that Our Lord entrusted his Mother to Saint John: "When Jesus saw his mother and the disciple there whom he loved, he said to his mother, 'Woman, behold, your son.' Then he said to the disciple, 'Behold, your mother.' And from that hour the disciple took her into his home" (Jn 19:26-27).

Catherine's sublime vision focuses on Mary. Catherine loves the Savior, the Lord Christ; she loves his cross; and she loves his Mother, the Blessed Virgin Mary. As Christ himself reveals from the cross, Mary stands out among the saints of God. She enjoys an efficacy that belongs to Christ's Mother alone. Catherine accordingly instructs us to envisage Mary as a "chariot," as a speedy carriage that brings into the world the Savior. "For," Catherine continues, "Mary is the intermediary, a real chariot of fire, who in conceiving within herself the Word, God's only-begotten Son, brought and gave [to us] the fire of love—for he is love itself."[32] These words that Jesus speaks, "Behold, your mother," confirm all that the Church holds authoritatively about the mediation of the Blessed Virgin Mary— in short, what the Church teaches about how Mary helps the rest of us, the Church on earth, get to heaven.

Mary ranks among the chosen instruments that God uses to communicate his love to the world. She ranks first among them, in fact. Catherine's mind turns to an agricultural metaphor. Just as plant life needs fertile soil in order to flourish, so Christ requires his human Mother. Mary, says Catherine, "was the field wherein was sown the seed of the incarnate Word, God's Son."[33] As Catherine continues her letter to a religious woman, a nun, a hermitess, who lived in the countryside outside of Florence, Catherine elaborates on her metaphor of Mary as a fertile field: "Truly, dearest sister, in that lovely blessed field the Word was engrafted into Mary's flesh as a seed is sown in the earth." Catherine explains in poetic language Galatians 4:4: "When the fullness of time had come, God sent his Son, born of a woman." Mary's mediation arises from her place as Mother of the Redeemer.

For his part, Saint John Paul II explains Mary's mediation in his encyclical letter titled *Redemptoris Mater*, Mother of the Redeemer: "Mary's mediation," says the encyclical, "*is intimately linked with her motherhood.* It possesses a specifically maternal character, which distinguishes it from the mediation of the other creatures who in various and always subordinate ways share in the one mediation of Christ."[34] Christ in this way places us before and entrusts us to the clement, the loving, the sweet Virgin Mary. As devout Catholics sing each evening at the end of the "Salve Regina," *O clemens, O pia, O dulcis Virgo Maria.* O clement, O loving, O sweet Virgin Mary.

Mary's maternal mediation, it is true, begins when the Eternal Word "by the Holy Spirit was incarnate of the Virgin Mary, and became man."[35] The Blessed Virgin Mary's vocation, however, also includes the sanctification of her human willing. We know that Mary clings to the divine command that God gives the Eternal Son. In order to stress that the human will of Mary remains perfectly united with that of her divine Son, Catherine resorts to dramatic imagery. She says that "[Mary] would have made a ladder of her very self to put her Son on the cross if there had been no other way."[36] This figure of speech—taken from spiritual authors familiar to Catherine—indicates the union of wills that binds Jesus and Mary. We should not pass lightly over this bond of loves. It teaches an important lesson: Nothing magical forms part of the divine plan. Nothing of the mechanical, the automatic, contributes to our salvation. No talismans. No totems. No shamans. The divine plan for our salvation includes only free participants. Because of her unique prerogatives, Mary abides the freest of us all, though she can choose only those things that God forcordains for her.

Christ himself establishes the model for this free self-giving when he says, again in the Gospel of John: "This is why the Father loves me, because I lay down my life in order to take it up again. No one takes it from me, but I lay it down on my own. I have power to lay it down, and power to take it up again. This command I have received from my Father" (Jn 10:17-18). To exhibit this truth in a purely human expression, God chose the Blessed Virgin Mary. She, who spoke her *Fiat* "with all her human and feminine 'I,'" stands forth as the most exquisite participant in the human drama of salvation.[37] So Catherine can assert boldly that Mary brings us "the fire and warmth of God's divine charity," and so also can she compare Mary to a rich field wherein the seed of God's Word is sown in order to blossom unto our salvation. "All this," insists Catherine, "because her Son's will remained in her."[38]

When Christ confides his Mother to the care of the disciple—"Woman, behold, your son"—he "[entrusts] humanity to the Mother of Christ."[39] When, in turn, Christ confides John to Mary—"Behold, your mother"—the dying Savior gives a fallen race the same precious gift of her person. "The Redeemer," says Saint John Paul II, "entrusts his mother to the disciple, and at the same time he gives her to him as his mother."[40] No Dominican saint would interpret this marvelous exchange of gifts as the last humanitarian gesture on the part of a dutiful son about to die. No Dominican saint would view Christ's instructions from his cross to disciple and Mother as a sweet detail added to an otherwise cruel historical narrative. The Dominican saint recognizes in this entrusting an expression of the divine plan of salvation that imposes itself upon every Christian believer. Christian iconography, as mentioned above, represents the Evangelist John as an eagle soaring heavenwards. In fact, Raymond of Capua, Catherine's guide and biographer, introduces his *Life* of the saint by explaining why John the Evangelist, John the Divine, appears as John the Eagle. As his explanation unfolds, Raymond of Capua enlarges on the reasons that Thomas Aquinas has given: "He [John] had soared in the Spirit to the peak of highest heaven," writes Raymond, "and was disclosing to the Church militant [the Church on earth] the secrets of God's plan."[41] No wonder Catherine exhorts us: "I want you to learn from that sweet mother Mary, who for God's honor and our salvation gave us her Son, dead on the wood of the most holy cross."[42] And Catherine also encourages us to invoke "the dear name of Mary, who is [our] advocate, the mother of grace and of mercy."[43] These are sublime mysteries of the Catholic religion that John the Evangelist communicates to the Church.[44]

CONSOLATION

"At noon darkness came over the whole land until three in the afternoon. And at three o'clock Jesus cried out in a loud voice, '*Eloi, Eloi, lema sabachthani?*' which is translated, 'My God, my God, why have you forsaken me?'" (Mk 15:33-34). Jesus speaks from the cross the word that, as it were, gives moment for pause. How, we may ask, could God abandon God? How could the Eternal Father abandon the Eternal Son? How could the God-Man, even as he hung from the cross, dying, proclaim in a pitiable outburst that sin had destroyed what the uncreated grace of the Incarnation had joined together? One divine Person, two natures, human and divine. Figuring out these riddles is simple: God did not abandon God. The Eternal Father did not separate himself from the Eternal Son become man. Sin by no means destroyed the hypostatic union—the technical expression that the Church employs to proclaim that the Incarnation of the Son of God remains forever.[45]

Still, we hear Jesus exclaim from the cross, "My God, my God, why have you forsaken me?" And upon hearing this cry ring out across the ages, who does not shudder? For by an analysis that unfolds almost instinctually in the Christian soul—really, in any person with even piecemeal self-knowledge—we wonder, "If God abandoned his only Son, whom even a criminal proclaimed an innocent victim, then what about me?" And from this well-meaning but faulty reasoning there follows a certain apprehension, a fright, a recoil. So we need a holy guide and a trustworthy interpreter to help us penetrate what remains one of the most examined texts of the New Testament. We need assistance in order to locate this cry of abandonment, this all-too-human emotion, within a context that illuminates its divine significance.

Although Catherine refers to Christ as abandoned on the cross, she does not advert directly to this cry. For Catherine, as for Aquinas and the tradition that follows him, the cry of abandonment requires a psychological analysis more than it does an elaborate, and at times overwrought, theological explanation. In other words, how can we illuminate the working of Christ's human consciousness in such a way that the cry of abandonment is not taken as a cry of despair? Overwrought theologians are not the only ones who jump upon these words of Jesus. Not a few rationalists—unbelieving interpreters of the New Testament they—take morose delight in this verse of the Christian Gospels. They interpret Christ's words as tantamount to his own admission of failure. For such *penseurs*, Christ dies an unhappy, self-deluded revolutionary. Were such impious thoughts, however, to reflect the true meaning of Christ's words, we of course would not find ourselves among more than a billion Catholic believers. Self-deluded revolutionaries do not survive for two millennia.

So we turn to our sister Catherine, who was not a professional theologian, and discover what the wisdom of the saints tells us about Christ's cry from the cross. In fact, Catherine provides a commentary that captures the general thinking of the Church about Christ's cry of abandonment. It runs like this: Christ, writes Catherine, "was both happy and sad on the cross. He was sad as he carried the cross of his suffering body and the cross of his longing to make satisfaction for the sin of humankind. And he was happy because his divine nature joined with his human nature could not suffer and made his soul always happy by showing itself to him unveiled. This is why he was at once happy and sad, because his flesh bore the pain the Godhead could not suffer—nor even his [human] soul, so far as the superior part of his intellect was concerned."[46] It sounds like a complicated explanation, but Catherine intends it for simple, not sophisticated, souls—for people like us. Catherine appeals to the psychology of Christ; that is, she explains how his human soul works. Each of us has known an experience in which the superior part of our mind has brought comfort to the sadness that we experience in the lower soul. For example, when a loved one dies, we experience sorrow. When at the same time we ponder in faith the everlasting life that Christ promises to those who die attached to him, we experience a surcease of unrelenting sorrow. What Christ knows in his human soul comes from his being the Incarnate Son of God. What we know—and it trumps even the most heartfelt sorrows—comes from our faith in those things that Christ has revealed, such as life everlasting. Faith knowledge can affect what we experience as suffering. Like Christ, the Christian can experience joy and sorrow at the same time.

What Saint Catherine calls "the superior part" of the intellect, we know simply as our reasonable self. Each time we recognize that human reason can smooth emotional upset, we find ourselves operating from what Catherine calls the "superior part" of our souls. Classical psychotherapy proceeds on the assumption that arranging the categories of an individual's personal understanding will relieve the various distresses and anxieties that afflict him or her. With sufficient time, skilled therapists can achieve some measure of success. On the cross, of course, Christ does not require counseling. Rather, the Incarnate Son continues to enjoy the full possession of the divine reason, even—nay, especially—after having mounted the wood of the cross. As Catherine reports God the Father speaking to her, "My beloved Son, your head, was the only one who could not grow in any sort of perfection, because he was one with me and I with him. His soul was beatified in his union with my divine nature."[47] How does this truth throw a light on Christ's cry of forsakenness? And, what is more important, how does it help us?

In his Palm Sunday homily at the beginning of Holy Week in 2011, Pope Benedict XVI reminded the Christian people of the situation in which those who inhabit the world find themselves. "The Fathers of the Church," he began, "maintained that human beings stand at the point of intersection between two gravitational fields. First, there is the force of gravity which pulls us down—towards selfishness, falsehood and evil; the gravity which diminishes us and distances us from the heights of God. On the other hand there is the gravitational force of God's love: the fact that we are loved by God and respond in love attracts us upwards."[48] The challenge of course arrives at the moment when we find ourselves pulled down, abandoned, when everything within our human psychology seems to scream out *Non serviam*—I will not serve.

At this juncture in our Christian lives—one moreover that can recur multiple times during a single lifetime—who among us would find great comfort in a savior who, in effect, had announced himself abandoned to "the force of gravity that pulls us down"? Would we not rather prefer to embrace a Savior who, though tested in every way, yet remained without sin? Would we not find better comfort in the Savior described in the Letter to the Hebrews? Catherine surely thought this verse from Hebrews—"For we do not have a high priest who is unable to sympathize with our weaknesses, but one who has similarly been tested in every way, yet without sin" (Heb 4:15)—explains best what happened to her gentle Christ when he felt abandoned on the cross.

And Catherine acts on this word. She tells Raymond of Capua and the Dominican priests he governs: "Go to the school of the Word, the Lamb slain and abandoned on the cross, because it is there that the true teaching is found."[49] To the leaders, the *Signori*, of Florence she proclaims that only the Church provides "the wedding garment we must have if we want to get into the wedding feast of eternal life, to which we are invited by the Lamb who was abandoned and slain on the cross for us."[50] To Pope Gregory XI, she writes, "I beg you, most holy father, for love of the Lamb who was slain, consumed, and abandoned on the cross: as his vicar fulfill this holy will of his by doing what you can"—that is, to leave Avignon and return to Rome.[51] And to a widowed noblewoman pondering whether or not to enter a monastery, Catherine encourages her "to follow the Lamb abandoned and consumed on the cross on his path of suffering, torment, disgrace, and insult."[52] Now consider this: Would these noble aspirations that Catherine encourages popes and Dominicans, political leaders and widowed noblewomen to pursue, thus imitating the "abandoned" Christ, make any sense whatsoever had this same Christ experienced a real abandonment by God? I think not. So let us follow Catherine's lead, her exegesis, and discover in Christ's cry of abandonment a source of strength for those moments when we suffer the strains of affective solitude, whenever, that is, we feel ourselves isolated from friends and family, or even from God.

ZEAL

The saints never tire of proclaiming to the
Church how much Jesus loves those whom he
has redeemed by his blood. They see in Christ's
thirst an expression of his zeal for souls. "After
this, aware that everything was now finished, in
order that the scripture might be fulfilled, Jesus
said, 'I thirst.' There was a vessel filled with
common wine. So they put a sponge soaked
in wine on a sprig of hyssop and put it up to
his mouth" (Jn 19:28-29). Jesus thirsts. Our
guide and companion, Catherine of Siena, offers a complete spiritual exegesis of this passage
from Saint John's Gospel. She explains this poi-
gnantly human appeal. "It seems," she writes,
"this is what he meant when he cried out on
the cross, 'I am thirsty!' as if to say, 'I have so
great a thirst for your salvation that I cannot
satisfy it: give me a drink!'" Jesus thirsts for
souls. Then Catherine continues, making a dis-
tinction: "The gentle Jesus was asking to drink
those he saw not sharing in the redemption
purchased by his blood, but he was given nothing to drink but bitterness. Ah, dearest father,"
continues Catherine, "not only at the time of

the crucifixion, but later and even now we continue to see him asking for this kind of drink, showing us that his thirst persists."[53] Catherine penned these words during the last quarter of the 14th century to an Italian prelate, Abbot Giovanni di Gano da Orvieto. Her words, however, retain their sense of urgency for all of us— prelates and priests, hermits and religious, lay men and women. The work of evangelization, as the recent popes have reminded us, falls on every member of the Church.

The message rings out clearly. Jesus continues to reach out to a sinful world. Christ's thirst for our salvation continues through the centuries. In the 17th century, God sent the message to a French nun of the Visitation. In turn, Saint Margaret Mary Alacoque (1647–90), with the indispensable help of her Jesuit confessor and director, Claude La Colombière (1641–82), spread worldwide the message of the Sacred Heart. What is the message of the Heart of Christ? Another expression of the "I thirst!" As we discover in the words that Jesus addresses to Margaret Mary, "Behold this Heart which has loved men so much that it has spared nothing, even to consuming itself."[54] In the 19th century, God communicated the "I thirst" message to another nun, the Carmelite Saint Thérèse of Lisieux (1873–97). She too understood Christ's cry from the cross as a plea for the salvation of souls, and Thérèse in turn encouraged countless millions of people to believe in Jesus' love for them no matter what their state. Though Thérèse Martin never left her Carmel in Normandy, her statue adorns practically every church in the United States, a sign of and testimony to the reception that her own spiritual doctrine, that of the "Little Way," has received among Christians everywhere. In the 20th century, God also delivered the same "I thirst" message to a Polish religious sister known today as Saint Faustina (1905–38). Her rendition of the familiar revelation has gained popularity under the rubric of the Divine Mercy, a devotion that Saint John Paul II introduced into the liturgical calendar on the Sunday immediately following Easter. And so it goes: Christ ensures that his message, his plea for souls, continues until he comes again to judge the living and the dead.

What may we conclude? If one considers the special recipients of Christ's "I thirst" message, we may suppose that God prefers to announce his thirst for souls through holy women. And is it not true? The feminine genius affords the best guarantee that a message meant to comfort the lowest and the poorest and the neediest of the human race will in fact reach them. Why? One expects to discover compassion in a woman. Everything that Catherine of Siena has taught us about Christ on the cross reveals her deep sense of the divine compassion and of its expression in the blood of Christ. Nevertheless, though her womanly compassion remains strong, Catherine refuses to coddle the lax soul. She gives no quarter to softness or self-indulgence or self-pity. Listen to the prayer that Catherine makes to Jesus: "*Oh sweetest, boundless, beloved charity! It was your infinite hunger and thirst for our salvation that made you cry out that you were thirsty! Though your agony there caused you intense physical thirst, your thirst for our salvation was even greater. Ah, ah me! There is no one to give you anything to drink except the bitterness of sin upon sin! How few there are who give you a drink freely and with pure loving affection!*"[55] Her estimate, I imagine, still holds good for our generation.

Catherine loves the Savior, our Lord Jesus Christ. She also loves his cross. She loves his Mother, Mary. Catherine loves the consolation that Christ's Passion introduces into the world. Catherine loves the blood of Christ, which washes away the stain of sin. Catherine loves the body of Christ, the Church. She assigns the first responsibility for the salvation of sinners to those to whom the Church confides the pastoral care of souls. When she addresses the prelates of her day, Catherine allows no reticence or reserve. "Run, run, venerable father!" she again writes to Abbot Giovanni di Gano da Orvieto. "No foolish irresponsibility, for time is short, and it is ours![56] And she tries to impress on the bishop of Florence, Angelo Ricasoli, a sense of urgency about seeking the divine compassion: "I beg you, my dearest cherished and venerable father, to rouse yourself from the sleep of indifference.... Give him [Christ] a drink, since he so graciously asks it of you."[57] Catherine empathizes with Christ's zeal for souls, his thirst for the salvation of every human being. She also understands what sinners need in order to become a worthy drink for Christ. So she urges the Church's pastors to take up energetically the work of evangelization, which includes the faithful administration of the sacraments. Catherine wants the whole world to slake Jesus' thirst. Christ thirsts for the souls of everyone. No human being stands excluded from receiving the gift of his compassionate blood.

Christ asks each human being for a drink. He shows himself thirsty for souls, zealous for their salvation. Each of our souls. The souls of those confided to our care. The souls of those whom we love. Even the souls of those whose salvation we may fear losing. "Oh unhappy me!" Catherine anguishes, "It seems to me that people give him [Christ] nothing but bitterness and the stench of sin!"[58] Catherine, however, never stops with a lament. She moves on. She exhorts, she encourages, she consoles.

Catherine loves the Church. She wants her friends to find a steady footing within the sacramental structures of the Church. Our Lord has placed within her heart the fervent desire, a burning zeal, to lead souls to himself. In order to fulfill this mission, Catherine must unmask the devil's blackmail, that subliminal taunt that makes us think that we will never change, never be good enough. So when she writes to a tailor's wife, Monna Agnesa, Catherine states plainly the way to satisfy the thirst of Jesus: "Bathe in the blood of Christ crucified. Hide yourself in his open side and make it your lovely dwelling place in holy knowledge of yourself and true knowledge of the generosity of his love."[59] When people complain that they lack the energy to extinguish Christ's thirst, Catherine proclaims the strong Lord. When others remark that their sinful selves cannot satisfy Christ's thirst, Catherine proclaims the merciful Lord. When still others wonder whether they know how to quench Christ's thirst, then Catherine responds,

"We can do everything through Christ crucified." Why? The answer is simple: "Our flesh," she explains to a young Italian nobleman involved in knight errantry and the passions that it provokes, "has been conquered by his flesh scourged, macerated, saturated with disgrace on the wood of the most holy cross, and in the end raised above all the choirs of angels in the resurrection of God's Son."[60] Catherine's convictions are clear: Each human being on earth can satisfy Jesus's thirst—even I. Even you.

THE POPE

"Then he joyously shouts, 'It is finished.' Yes, those seem to be sorrowful words, but they were words of joy to that soul aflame and consumed in the fire of divine charity, the soul of the Incarnation of the Word, God's Son. It is as if the gentle Jesus wanted to say, 'I have completely fulfilled what was written of me. Fulfilled too is my painful desire to redeem the human race. I am happy, exultant, that I have finished this suffering. I have fulfilled the commission given me by my Father, a commission I so longed to accomplish.'"[61] Thus Catherine helps us to understand that Christ sees his death as a completion, not as an end. "When Jesus had taken the wine, he said, 'It is finished.' And bowing his head, he handed over the spirit" (Jn 19:30).

We find ourselves caught up in Catherine's buoyant enthusiasm. At the same time, we discover that Catherine's joy imitates the Lord's own. So our guide and companion hears Christ saying: "I am happy, exultant, that I have finished this suffering. I have fulfilled the commission given me by my Father, a commission

I so longed to accomplish." Catherine continues her commentary on these words of the Savior: "When the Word, God's dear Son, received the great command from his Father, he ran as one in love to the shameful death of the most holy cross. By fulfilling this command he fulfilled the truth—that is, we were, from God's perspective, restored to grace if we would only not kick back with our wretchedness and sin."[62] Note well the order of Catherine's exegesis, which reflects her Dominican training: Dominicans look first to Christ and his truth, and then to their own impurities, their wretchedness. We should most fear losing Christ's gift of salvation. Holy fear suffices then to keep us from kicking back with our wretchedness and sin.

Christians learn from Saint Augustine to associate the moment of Christ's Death with the birth of the Church. "For it was from the side of Christ as he slept the sleep of death upon the cross that there came forth the 'wondrous sacrament of the whole Church.'"[63] Catherine rejoices when she ponders what the sacraments of the Church accomplish in us. Christ's life on earth is finished. Catherine can only marvel at what follows upon the shedding of his compassionate blood. "In that blood we were washed clean of sin in holy baptism," she explains to the queen of Naples, "and he has gathered all of us Christians together in the garden of holy Church. Consider that no one other than our mother, holy Church, has given them [the supporters of the antipope] this cleansing or these glorious roses, and she has given them through the supreme pontiff...who holds the keys to the blood."[64] Catherine laments those who have rebelled against the legitimate pope, Urban VI, even as she affirms the union of pope and sacraments. So she asks the queen to consider that those who separate themselves from the Church defile the sacramental gifts, especially Baptism and the Eucharist, that God has given them through the same Church. Catherine's images still capture the imagination. The cleansing waters of Baptism and the "glorious roses" of the sacramental graces that find their source in Christ's blood. These sacraments belong to the Church, and to the legitimate pope, "who holds the keys to the blood" and to the other gifts of salvation that flow from the pierced side of Christ.[65]

We understand better Catherine's passionate love for the Church when we recall that she lived during a period when enormous confusion reigned in the Church, a period that historians refer to as the Babylonian captivity of the papacy (1309–77) and the Western Schism (1378–1417). This schism—which erupted after the Italian Urban VI was elected to succeed the Frenchman Gregory XI divided the allegiances of Catholic Europe among two and then three claimants to the papal throne. The disagreement was resolved only by the abdication of the pope and the two antipopes and the election of a new, legitimate pope, Martin V (1369–1431), who won the allegiance of all. At the same time, it proves useful to recall that Catherine expended much of her spiritual energy in an effort to restore one pope to his rightful place in the city of Rome and then to maintain him there. For this reason, in 1939, Pope Pius XII named her, along with Saint Francis of

Assisi, as a co-patron of Italy.[66] What we find instructive, however, is that Catherine would suffer no division within the Church. What Christ united under Peter (see Mt 16:18), he intended should remain united under the authority of one earthly head. Catherine, in words reminescent of the confession of John the Baptist (see Jn 1:20), wrote: "I proclaim and do not deny that you are the vicar of Christ," she wrote to Pope Urban VI. "You are the cellarer who holds the keys to the wine cellar of holy Church in which is the blood of the humble spotless Lamb."[67] The perennial lesson that Catherine offers today's Catholics exposes the indispensable mediation of the hierarchal Church in the divine plan that governs our salvation. Without a trace of ambiguity, the Second Vatican Council makes this claim: "In order to shepherd the People of God and to increase its numbers without cease, Christ the Lord set up in his Church a variety of offices which aim at the good of the whole body."[68] At the center of the worldwide communion that we call the Church still stands the pope, the bishop of Rome, "visible source and foundation" of the Church's unity.[69] No wonder Catherine scolds a ranking nobleman, the count of Fondi, who had turned against Pope Urban VI to support the antipope, Clement: "How can you do," she confronted him, "what you shouldn't be doing against your head."[70]

Catherine loves the Savior, his cross, his Mother, his mystical body, the Church, and the bishop of Rome, the pope. Little wonder that she writes to the queen of Naples, Giovanna d'Angiò, who herself had gone over to the Avignon obedience of the antipope Clement: "Show yourself a faithful daughter of sweet holy Church. For you know that she is a mother who feeds her children at her breast with sweetest life-giving milk."[71] Catherine affirms that the true Church and her lawful ministers alone can dispense what the saint metaphorically describes as the mother's milk of sound instruction and the sacraments. Catherine's insistence on the visible institutes of the Church provides a salutary reminder to our era, in which so many are prone to relativizing—that is, to discounting—the importance of both the Church's hierarchy and her sacraments.

Catherine deeply understood the relationship of the hierarchical structure of the Church to the communication of the divine benefits that Christ's Death inaugurates. In other words, she knew that the divine graces that Christ obtains by his Death on the cross reach us, the intended beneficiaries, through the Church's pastors and her sacraments. So she warns those who distance themselves from the pope. To the rebellious political leaders of Florence, she appeals: "You know well that Christ left us his vicar, and he has left him as a help for our souls. There is nowhere we can have salvation except in the mystic body of holy Church, whose head is Christ and whose members we are. Whoever disobeys Christ on earth, who takes the place of Christ in heaven, will have no share in the fruit of the blood of God's Son. For God has decreed that through his hands the blood will be communicated and given to us, as well as all the sacraments of holy Church, which receive life from this blood."[72] What Catherine said to these 14th-century Florentine political authorities, holds true for us today. The successor of Peter, the pope, abides as the perpetual source and foundation of the Church's unity and ministry. He serves as "pastor of the entire Church."

PRIESTS

Christ's final commendation moves Catherine
to ponder the plight of those who live without
proper pastoral care. "It was now about noon
and darkness came over the whole land until
three in the afternoon because of an eclipse of
the sun. Then the veil of the temple was torn
down the middle. Jesus cried out in a loud
voice, 'Father, into your hands I commend my
spirit'; and when he had said this he breathed
his last" (Lk 23:44-46). Catherine in fact provides us with her own interpretation of this final word that Jesus speaks from the cross. "It
seems," she writes, "this is what the dear mouth
of Truth meant on the wood of the most holy
cross when he said, 'Into your hands, Lord, I
commend my spirit' (Lk 23:46). *Oh gentle Jesus,
you are in the Father, but we were not, because
like gangrenous members we were deprived of grace
by sin.*"[73] Catherine chooses to impress upon us
the dramatic situation facing those who do not
enjoy an active union with Christ. Note that
she refers to Christ as the "mouth of Truth."
Catherine knows that the greatest harm that can
befall the human creature is ignorance. Man,

who is made to know the truth, suffers most when he is deprived of the truth. The remedy for this circumstance requires that one receive a messenger of truth, a prophet, a pastor, a priest. Otherwise, as the image of gangrene suggests, ignorance of Christ progressively results in the corruption of the whole person.

Is it not the case? Think about it: philosophical outlooks on life—outlooks that do not advert to the truth of Christ—bear up badly, especially when they are placed under the pressure of those human sufferings that no one escapes. A person, true enough, may adopt an optimistic air, and so dismiss human tragedy as a perspectival problem. On this account, one need only adjust one's mental categories to make the distress disappear. The power of positive thinking, however, goes only so far. No one passes through life without some suffering, including the final suffering which is death.

Or, secondly, a person may opt for pessimism, moving from day to day and always anticipating the worst. To survive in this way, one needs to maintain a stoic attitude, to grin and bear the hard knocks that come every day. When this stoicism fails, however, the pessimist is left to succumb to depression, despair, or both. These postures inhibit the native drive for happiness or fulfillment that characterizes the human creature. Saint Thomas teaches us that all men seek happiness; only a madman works to make himself unhappy.

Nihilism appears as a third alternative to one's having confidence in the compassionate blood of Christ. The nihilist eschews moral limits and creates his own value system. Nihilism, even when it is fashionably displayed by devil-may-care inhabitants of dark subcultures, cannot satisfy the human spirit. No one can completely detach himself from the reality of the created order. The intelligibility that God has inscribed in both spirit and matter survives all efforts to frustrate it. At the end of the day, radical nihilists destroy themselves.

Since none of these outlooks acknowledge God's loving providence, little wonder that Catherine describes as "gangrenous" those who do not enjoy an active union with Christ—the implacable optimist, the stoic pessimist, and the freewheeling nihilist. Each of these must be, in a word, cut off: cut off from truth, cut off from love.

Catherine does not want to see her children sad; her meditations offer good news. Good news for those who heed her counsels, good news for those who have entered any Catholic church to draw near to Christ's cross, good news for those who place their hope and faith in the Lord Christ. She wants us to find the way out of the world's web of lies: to discover a way out of the labyrinth of naive and unsustainable optimism, to discover a way out of the maze of stark and uncaring stoicism, to discover a way out of "no-exit" moral relativism. This Way, Catherine insists, gushes forth from the pierced side of Christ, at the moment when he commends his spirit into the hands of his Father in heaven. Catherine allows no one to despair, "I am a sinner and have lost the way." "For," she assures us, "if all the sins there are were collected in my one body, and I still had true hope and lively faith in infinite mercy, nobody would be able to keep me from receiving and sharing in the fruit of the compassionate blood of God's Son, which the gentle Jesus shed to fulfill the Father's command and to save us."[74]

Catherine loves the gentle Jesus; she loves his cross; she loves his Mother, sweet Mary. Catherine loves the consolation that Jesus and Mary bring; she loves the blood of Christ; she loves the Church and its "head," the pope. Catherine also loves priests. Even the bad ones. To manifest her love, she would write to them. For example, to the parish priest of Asciano, a village about 25 kilometers outside Siena, she pens these striking words: "Oh dearest father, give a little thought to your perilous state! In what great danger you are, drowning in this bitter sea of deadly sin!... Let's not be naive: it is the height of stupidity to make oneself deserving of death when one could have life."[75] Catherine exhibits love toward wayward priests. She can also display candor, as when she writes to Pope Urban VI: "Oh wretched me, I say it sorrowfully! Your sons are feeding on what they receive through their ministry of the blood of

Christ, and they aren't ashamed to act as gamblers, playing their games with those holy hands anointed by you, Christ's vicar!"[76] Catherine's concern to point out the faults of priests leads her to encourage priests to remain mindful of their dignity within the Church. And so to another parish priest, Andrea de' Vitroni, she says, "I long to see you enlightened with true, most perfect light, so that you may know the dignity in which God has placed you. For without light you would be unable to know this."[77] It is a reminder that every priest must heed.

Catherine loves priests, even as she detests the abuses that she has observed them commit within the visible structures of the Church. "Do not tolerate the act of impurity," she instructs Pope Urban VI. "Tolerate neither simony nor grand ceremonies nor entertainments, nor gambling with blood…as they [priests] set up their gambling tables in the place that should be God's temple!"[78] For all her straightforwardness, however, Catherine never loses sight of the gift and mystery that Christ's priesthood embodies. She recognizes the irreplaceable and indispensable office that priests enjoy within the Church. "Priests," she reminds us, "are assigned within the mystic body of holy Church to administer to us the body and blood of Christ crucified."[79] With the Eucharist come the other sacraments, as well as every spiritual gift that is required in order that the Eucharist occupy the center of each human life. Among these spiritual gifts stand first of all the theological and the infused moral virtues. So Catherine helped the young men of her own period to grow in virtue. Today also, through her spiritual doctrine, she would encourage young men thinking about a priestly vocation to embrace a life of Christian virtue and to frequent the sacrament of penance. She would further urge suitably disposed men to offer themselves as candidates for the priesthood. Who else but the priest, she would ask, can "administer to us the body and blood of Christ crucified"? Because they act in the person of Christ, Catherine allows for no softness. "Ministers especially," she again tells Andrea de' Vitroni, "whom supreme Goodness calls his christs, ought to be angels and not mere human beings."[80]

Because of her affiliation with the *Mantellate*, a group of pious women associated with the Dominican Order, Catherine demonstrated a special benevolence toward the Order of Preachers. After Raymond of Capua had become her confessor and guide, Catherine took on the task of keeping the Dominican Order in sound spiritual shape. Christ's final commendation from the cross, his handing over of his spirit, speaks directly to Dominican life, for Dominicans imitate their holy father, Saint Dominic, by reposing complete confidence in the Providence of God. They always commend their spirits to the workings of God's wise and loving Providence, firm in the expectation that by holy obedience they will achieve their own sanctification and the salvation of souls. God himself taught Catherine the all-important lesson of reposing in his Providence, of commending her spirit to his wisdom and love. Consider, says the Eternal Father to Catherine, the example of your father Saint Dominic, "who trusting by the light of faith that I would provide," told his sons to sit at table although there was no food in the house to eat. "Then I who provide for those who trust in me sent two angels with the whitest of bread, so much that they had great plenty for several weeks."[81] This miracle that God worked at the prayers of Saint Dominic still sustains his sons and daughters. And so Catherine encourages us to commend our lives into the care of this wise and loving Providence, and to find the opportune helps for this daily commendation from the Church's priests, whose sacramental identity sustains a fallen world.

COMPASSIONATE
BLOOD

‿◦~◦~◦~◦~◦~◦~◦~◦~

Jesus' cross and Passion return us to our beginnings, to the beginning of the world's history, when, through pride and disobedience, sinful Adam rebelled against the plan of the divine wisdom. As Saint Paul writes to the Corinthians, "For just as in Adam all die, so too in Christ shall all be brought to life" (1 Cor 15:22). They return us also to the beginning of Christian history, for in the liturgy of the Annunciation the Church places on Christ's lips the words of the fortieth psalm, "To do your will, O my God, is my delight, and your law is within my heart!" (cf. Ps 40:9). Catherine's meditation on the Passion of Christ unveils the benefits that the world receives from the shed blood of God's only Son. "And because his only will was to do his Father's will," writes Catherine to some monks, "all the pain, torment, scorn, and death were turned for him into the greatest sweetness—so much so that coming to his sufferings seemed to him like coming to a Pasch."[82] She means like "coming to a joyful Passover feast" (cf. Lk 22:15). While Catherine grieves the sufferings that Christ underwent during his

Passion, she unfailingly points out the graces that this Passion brings. Catherine grasped the significance of the New Testament text that the Church reads at Easter: "Think of what is above, not of what is on earth" (Col 3:2). So Saint Paul urges the Colossians.

In one of her earliest letters, Catherine addresses her gentle Jesus with this prayer: "Oh sweetest treasured love! I can see not another answer for us but the sword that you, dearest love, had in your own heart and soul. That sword was your hatred for sin and your love for the Father's honor and our salvation. Oh sweetest love, this was the sword that struck your mother's heart and soul."[83] Catherine loves her Savior, her dearest and crucified Jesus. Catherine loves his holy and sweet cross. Catherine loves his gentle Mother, Mary, who remained by his cross. Catherine loves the consolation that the cross of Christ brings to the world. Catherine loves the missionary zeal that animates and compels those who discover the mystery of Christ's compassionate blood. Catherine loves the pope, our holy father, the vicar of Christ and head of the Church on earth. Catherine loves the priests whom the pope sends and who remain in communion with him. What is most important, Catherine loves each member of the Church who practices a true devotion to the Passion of Christ; she also loves those who want to appreciate what the compassionate blood of Christ bestows on the world. To what end does Catherine love the mysteries of Christ's Passion and those who embrace them? Catherine desires that those who join her circle of followers "live and grow in grace and in the end live in the eternal vision of God."[84] We see this desire illustrated in the spiritual counsel that she offers to those who seek out her friendship.

Late in the year of 1376, Catherine of Siena wrote to a young Sienese man, Stefano di Corrada Maconi. Even today, Stefano stands out as a recognizable figure. He aspired to live a Christian life, even the life of a monk, but he grew weary of his sinful weaknesses, especially his failures in observing holy purity. The excitements that easily distract adolescent males left Stefano doubtful that he could sustain his religious aspirations, that he could even live a holy life. To make matters worse, it seems that his family, especially his mother, Monna Giovanna, would have preferred that he follow a bourgeois life. Stefano, however, was drawn to Catherine and her charismatic circle of friends, and he joined them. He even accompanied Catherine to Avignon. She in turn showed a special interest in the young Stefano and took care to see that he learned the mystery of Christ's compassionate blood. Catherine taught Stefano how to live by faith in the blood of Christ. He then became the privileged beneficiary not only of Catherine's spiritual instruction but of her personal communication, of her friendship.

"Dearest son in Christ gentle Jesus," Catherine begins her letter to Stefano.[85] She then encourages him to persevere in the holy instruction that he has received from her. Catherine knows the soul of Stefano. She anticipates his demurral. His complaint sounds like the complaints that many Catholics today still voice: virtue proves too difficult to sustain. "But you will say to me," writes Catherine, "'How can I have this sort of strength, since I am so weak and frail that every little thing knocks me down?'" To Catherine's mind, Stefano suffers from the devil's blackmail. The devil's blackmail produces its poisonous effect when sinners capitulate to the proposal that, since they are sinners, no remedy exists for their dilemma, and so they must remain sinners. The blackmailed soul stands convinced that Jesus came to save somebody else. Catherine shows herself well practiced in unmasking this primordial lie. "My answer," she replies to Stefano, "is, I admit you are weak and frail so far as your sensuality is concerned, but not so when it comes to reason and spiritual strength." Catherine reminds Stefano of two aids to developing moral rectitude available to the Christian believer. The first is a natural truth, one knowable even to philosophers, whereas the second is a supernatural truth that only the saints comprehend. The natural truth holds that knowledge of what is right can affect the doing of what is right. Truth, in other words, provides the first effective remedy against the commission of a mortal sin. Admittedly, knowledge is not virtue; however, knowledge provides the seeds of virtue. The supernatural truth offers more. When a person knows the truth and also believes in the power of God's grace to make the truth effective in his or her life, then human reasoning receives an added assistance. "For in Christ's blood we are made strong," Catherine assures us, "even though weakness persists in our sensuality."

Catherine's remedy for moral weakness exhibits the distinctively Dominican emphasis that Aquinas places on the power of human intelligence not only to guide but also to strengthen human conduct. To grasp this distinctiveness, observe the complete absence of moralism in Catherine's spiritual exhortations. Note well that Catherine does not say to the perplexed Stefano, "Try harder!" Instead she counsels him to recognize that he and others can "gain this glorious virtue of strength and steady perseverance since our reason is made strong in Christ's blood." What must one do? "We must drown ourselves in this sweet glorious ransom." The language of ransom reminds us that Christ shed his compassionate blood on the cross in order to save the human race from thralldom to the devil. Indeed, therein lies the profound reason for referring to the blood of Christ as "compassionate." Had God not shown compassion toward the human race, we would have remained in a very sorry state. No wonder that Catherine interrupts her letter to Stefano in order to address Jesus himself: "Oh compassionate blood, through you was distilled compassionate mercy!" Catherine addresses the blood of Christ. She wants Stefano to realize that he can think of himself as enjoying a personal relationship with the blood of Christ. "Oh sweet blood," she ecstatically cries out, "you strip us of the selfish sensual love that weakens those who wear it, and you clothe us in the fire of divine charity."

We do not enjoy the physical presence of Catherine of Siena as did Stefano Maconi. However, we do enjoy her spiritual companionship. Each one of us can cry out, Catherine, my Mother![86] Pray for us. Intercede for us. Draw us close to your sweet Jesus. "He is such a loving companion to souls that follow him," Catherine assures us, "that when we reach the end in death, he puts us to rest in that bed, that peaceful sea of divine Being, where we receive the eternal vision of God. It seems this is what the dear mouth of Truth meant on the wood of the most holy cross when he said, 'Into your hands, Lord, I commend my spirit.'"[87] Or as Catherine herself spoke the phrase, "*In manus tuas, Domine, commendo spiritum meum.*"

NOTES

Notes

1. This is reported by her Dominican biographer Raymond of Capua, in his *Life of Catherine of Siena*, trans. Conleth Kearns, O.P. (Wilmington, Del.: Michael Glazier, Inc., 1980), no. 348, pp. 322–23.

2. *Letters of Catherine of Siena*, IV, 367. (See note 5 below for publication information on the *Letters*.)

3. Raymond of Capua, *Life*, no. 347, p. 322.

4. See Dominico Beccafumi, *Saint Catherine of Siena Receiving the Stigmata*, Domenico Beccafumi (c. 1513–15), oil and gold on wood, 11 ¼ in. x 16 ¼ in.

5. Catherine of Siena, *The Dialogue*, trans. Suzanne Noffke, O.P. (New York: Paulist Press, 1980); *The Letters of Catherine of Siena*, trans. Suzanne Noffke, O.P. Volume I was published in 1988 by the Center for Medieval and Early Renaissance Studies in Binghamton, N.Y. Volumes II–IV were published from 2001 to 2008 by the Arizona Center for Medieval and Renaissance Studies [ACMRS] in Tempe, Ariz. Citations to the *Letters* give volume and page numbers.

6. *Letters* II, 323.

7. *Letters* II, 323-24.

8. T. S. Eliot, *Four Quartets*, no. 2, "East Coker," I: "In my beginning is my end."

9. *Letters* I, 263.

10. The play aired in January 1962 on NBC-TV, an episode of the production "The Catholic Hour," then filmed in New York City. For the script, see the April 1962 issue of the Dominican magazine *The Torch*, pp. 23–31.

11. *Letters* I, 238. Catherine addresses these words to the 14th-century French king Charles V (1338–80).

12. *Catechism of the Catholic Church (CCC)* 405.

13. Flannery O'Connor, "The Fiction Writer and His Country," in Flannery O'Connor, *Collected Works*, ed. Sally Fitzgerald (New York: The Library of America, 1988), p. 805.

14. *Letters* III, 140.

15. Oscar Wilde, *The Ballad of Reading Gaol*, IV (New York: Brentano's, 1909).

16. *Letters* I, 272.

17. *Letters* II, 459. Catherine enlarges on Rom 8:18.

18. See *Summa theologiae* IaIIae q. 112, a. 1, ad 1.

19. *Letters* I, 73.

20. *Letters* I, 73.

21. See Hans Urs von Balthasar, *The Office of Peter and the Structure of the Church*, trans. Andrée Emery (San Francisco: Ignatius Press, 1974), pp. 301–7. I acknowledge the work of Jesuit Father John McIntyre for this reference; see his "Flannery O'Connor, un inventaire," *Pierre d'Angle* 17 (2011): 87–102.

22. *Letters* I, 73.

23. *Letters* I, 73.

24. See *Summa theologiae* IIIa q. 48, a. 2.

25. *Letters* I, 73.

26. *Letters* I, 73.

27. T. S. Eliot, *Four Quartets*, no. 1, "Burnt Norton," II.

28. Exultet, *Roman Missal*.

29. *Letters* I, 220. See also III, 168; IV, 368: "And now I am begging and urging you, father and son given to me by that dear mother Mary...."

30. This city in southern France provided a refuge for popes during a period of political and ecclesiastical turbulence that left the Italian peninsula unstable.

31. Raymond of Capua, *Life*, Prologue 1, p. 1. See also *Letters* I, 342, n. 6.

32. *Letters* II, 313.

33. *Letters* I, 117.

34. *Redemptoris Mater* 38; emphasis added.

35. Nicene Creed, *Roman Missal*.

36. *Letters* I, 118.

37. *Redemptoris Mater* 13.

38. *Letters* I, 118.

39. *Redemptoris Mater* 45.

40. *Redemptoris Mater* 45: "The Redeemer entrusts his mother to the disciple, and at the same time he gives her to him as his mother. Mary's motherhood, which becomes man's inheritance, is a gift: a gift which Christ himself makes personally to every individual. The Redeemer entrusts Mary to John because he entrusts John to Mary. At the foot of the Cross there begins that special entrusting of humanity to the Mother of Christ, which in the history of the Church has been practiced and expressed in different ways."

41. Raymond of Capua, *Life*, Prologue 1, p. 1

42. *Letters* II, 249–50.

43. *Letters* II, 313.

44. Other saints will even speak about the "secret of Mary." See, for example, Louis-Marie Grignion de Montfort's *Le Secret de Marie*. English translation: *The Secret of Mary* (London: Burns Oates & Washbourne, 1926).

45. See *CCC* 467.

46. *Dialogue*, p. 146.

47. *Dialogue*, p. 166.

48. Pope Benedict XVI, "Homily on Palm Sunday," 2011.

49. *Letters* II, 5.

50. *Letters* II, 142.

51. *Letters* II, 235.

52. *Letters* II, 369.

53. *Letters* I, 210.

54. H. J. Heagney, *"Behold This Heart": The Story of St. Margaret Mary Alacoque* (New York: P. J. Kenedy & Sons, 1947), p. 332.

55. *Letters* I, 125. Where Catherine is speaking to Christ, the editor of her *Letters* has put her words in italic type.

56. *Letters* I, 210.

57. *Letters* I, 125.

58. *Letters* I, 210.

59. *Letters* III, 207–8.

60. *Letters* I, 152.

61. *Letters* I, 88.

62. *Letters* IV, 244.

63. *CCC* 1067, citing Augustine's *Expositions on the Psalms* 138, 2.

64. *Letters* IV, 225.

65. *Roman Missal*, Preface for the Mass in honor of the Most Sacred Heart of Jesus: "[Christ] poured out blood and water from his pierced side, the wellspring of the Church's Sacraments."

66. On June 18, 1939, Pope Pius XII named Francis a joint Patron Saint of Italy along with Saint Catherine of Siena with the apostolic letter *Licet Commissa*, *AAS* XXXI (1939): 256–57. Pius XII mentioned the two saints in the laudative discourse he pronounced on May 5, 1949, in the Santa Maria sopra Minerva Church.

67. *Letters* III, 284. That Urban VI remains buried in St Peter's Basilica signals his place among the legitimate pontiffs of the Catholic Church.

68. See *CCC* 874, citing *Lumen gentium* 18.

69. See *CCC* 882, citing *Lumen gentium* 23.

70. *Letters* IV, 332.

71. *Letters* I, 136.

72. *Letters* IV, 214.

73. *Letters* I, 104.

74. *Letters* I, 256.

75. *Letters* I, 57.

76. *Letters* III, 153.

77. *Letters* III, 275–76.

78. *Letters* III, 215.

79. *Letters* III, 257.

80. *Letters* III, 277.

81. *Dialogue*, p. 314.

82. *Letters* I, 256.

83. *Letters* I, 38.

84. *Letters* I, 153.

85. All quotations in this paragraph come from Catherine's *Letters* I, 262. Those in the next paragraph are from her *Letters* I, 263.

86. Again we borrow this phrase from the title of the 1962 television play by Dominic Rover, o.p., *Catherine, My Mother*.

87. *Letters* I, 103–4. The phrase occurs in the breviary, as a responsory at Compline.